Hammered by a HEAT WAVE!

Disaster SURVIVORS

by Laura DeLallo

Consultants:

Daphne Thompson, Meteorologist
Educational Outreach Coordinator
Cooperative Institute for Mesoscale Meteorological Studies
National Weather Center

Keith C. Heidorn, Ph.D.
CMOS Accredited Consulting Meteorologist (retired)
Publisher and Editor of *The Weather Doctor* Web site

BEARPORT
PUBLISHING

New York, New York

Credits
Cover © Marc Romanelli/The Image Bank/Getty Images, and © Duncan Frazier/Shutterstock; Title Page, © Duncan Frazier/Shutterstock; TOC, © Keith Tarrier/Shutterstock; 4, © Patrick Frilet/Hemis/Alamy; 5, © AP Images/MTI/ Zsolt Szigetvary; 6, © Randy Wells Photography; 7T, © Ralf-Finn Hestoft/Corbis; 7B, © Kim Karpeles/Alamy; 8-9, © Jean Ayissi/AFP/Getty Images; 9, © AP Images/P. Anil Kumar; 10, © Yawar Nazir/Getty Images; 11T, © Andre Jenny/Alamy; 11B, © Stephen Brashear/Getty Images; 12, © Uli Seit/The New York Times/Redux; 13, © Ilza De Wet/iStockphoto; 14, © Jason Kempin/Redux; 15, © AP Images/Paul Sakuma; 16, © Zhao Peng/Xinhua/Landov; 17, © Justin Sullivan/Getty Images; 18, © Kevin C. Cox/Getty Images; 21, © Bruno Vincent/Getty Images; 22-23, © Pedro Armestre/AFP/Getty Images; 23, © Pedro Armestre/AFP/Getty Images; 24, © AP Images/Chicago Department of Environment/Mark Farina; 25, © Alexander Chaikin/Shutterstock; 26, © Spencer Grant/PhotoEdit, Inc.; 27, © Tim Boyle/Getty Images; 28L, © Sherwin Crasto/Reuters/Landov; 28R, © Tim Wimborne/Reuters/Landov; 29T, © David R. Frazier Photolibrary, Inc./ Alamy; 29B, © Alan Myers/Alamy.

Publisher: Kenn Goin
Editorial Director: Adam Siegel
Creative Director: Spencer Brinker
Design: Dawn Beard Creative
Photo Researcher: Amy Dunleavy

Library of Congress Cataloging-in-Publication Data

DeLallo, Laura.
  Hammered by a heat wave! / by Laura DeLallo ; consultants, Daphne Thompson, Keith C. Heidorn.
      p. cm. — (Disaster survivors)
  Includes bibliographical references and index.
  ISBN-13: 978-1-936087-51-8 (lib. bdg.)
  ISBN-10: 1-936087-51-0 (lib. bdg.)
  1. Heat waves (Meteorology)—Juvenile literature. I. Title.
  QC981.8.A5D45 2010
  551.5'253—dc22
                              2009043180

For more information, write to Bearport Publishing Company, Inc., 101 Fifth Avenue, Suite 6R, New York, New York 10003. Printed in the United States of America in North Mankato, Minnesota.

122009
090309CGE

10 9 8 7 6 5 4 3 2 1

Contents

The Race Is On

On the morning of July 15, 1995, ambulance driver Michelle McInnis raced across Chicago. For the third day in a row, the temperature was about to soar past 98°F (37°C). The extreme heat had caused a woman at a funeral to pass out. Michelle picked her up and sped toward a hospital where doctors could help her.

An ambulance speeding through Chicago, Illinois

Before Michelle reached the hospital, she heard the **dispatchers** speaking on the radio. They frantically asked drivers if they were free to pick up more sick people. "This is crazy," Michelle said to her ambulance partner. People all over Chicago were getting sick from the heat.

Rescue workers help a patient who is ill from the heat.

On July 13, 1995, the temperature hit 106°F (41°C) at Chicago's Midway Airport. It was the second hottest July day in recorded Chicago history.

Staying Cool

For nearly 24 hours, Michelle zipped across the city in her ambulance, rescuing people who were deathly ill from the heat. Michelle felt sick, too. The air conditioner in her ambulance had stopped working. "I was overwhelmed by the heat," she said. There was no time for Michelle to worry about herself, however. She had lives to save.

People cooled off at beaches during the 1995 Chicago heat wave.

While Michelle worked, people all over the city tried to find ways to stay cool. Many stayed indoors where there was air-conditioning. Some people headed to local beaches, where they could cool off in the water. Others opened **fire hydrants** and let the cool water spray them.

Chicago children play in the cold water coming from a fire hydrant.

People in Chicago opened more than 3,000 fire hydrants during the **heat wave**. City workers rushed around to close them. They needed the water for fire emergencies.

Sick in the City

The extreme heat in Chicago lasted for four days. It made thousands of people sick. Hospitals could not handle the large number of **patients**. They ran out of supplies and rooms. Dr. Leslie Zun remembers looking around an emergency room filled with patients. "This is real bad," he thought.

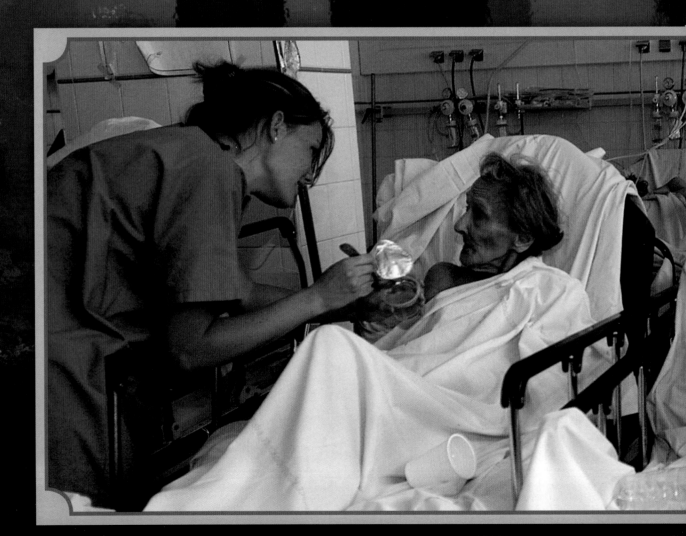

Not long into her **shift**, Michelle realized how bad it was, too. She worked long stretches with no breaks. Many people were already dead when she reached them. After rescuing people for almost 24 hours, she was exhausted. "I went home and I cried," she later said. By the time the city began to cool down, the heat had killed about 700 people.

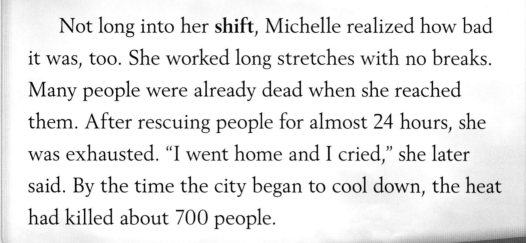

Doctors give patients lots of liquids and cold foods to help them recover from heat illnesses.

Other U.S. cities experienced very high temperatures in July 1995. On July 28 the temperature reached 121°F (49°C) in Phoenix, Arizona—the second-hottest day in Phoenix ever recorded.

Hot Enough to Kill

From July 12 to July 15, 1995, Chicago suffered through the deadly heat wave. Each year, heat waves kill more people than any other kind of weather disaster.

Average Number of Weather-Related Deaths per Year in the United States: 1998–2007

	0	25	50	75	100	125	150	175
Heat								
Hurricanes								
Floods								
Tornadoes								
Lightning								

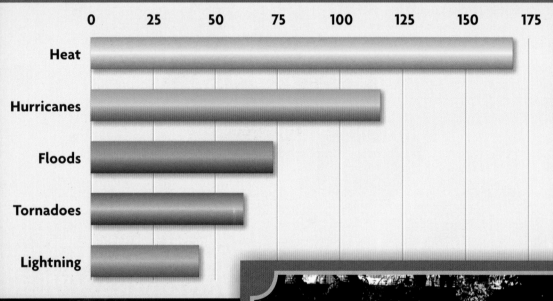

People share a small spot of shade to try to get some relief from a heat wave.

When is it hot enough to call a stretch of hot days a heat wave? Not all **meteorologists** agree. Many, however, say a heat wave is when summer temperatures reach about 10 degrees Fahrenheit (5 degrees Celsius) above the normal high for several days in a row. In July, temperatures in Chicago usually reach a high of around 83.5°F (28.6°C). During the 1995 heat wave, daily high temperatures ranged from about 94 to 106°F (34 to 41°C).

During a heat wave, some people cool off in a city's fountains.

One of the deadliest weather disasters in the northeastern United States was the 11-day heat wave of 1911. Almost 400 people died as temperatures soared past 100°F (38°C).

Sweat It Out

Heat waves are deadly because people can get sick or die if their bodies become too hot. The normal human body temperature is 98.6°F (37°C). When the body temperature rises to 104°F (40°C) or higher, important **organs** like the heart and kidneys can stop working correctly. Luckily, the body has a way to keep itself cool.

People who work outside are especially at risk of getting sick during a heat wave.

A person's body sweats when it is hot. Sweating is the release of some of the water in the body through the skin. As the liquid **evaporates**, the skin cools. If a person's body does not have enough liquids, it cannot sweat and cool off. The person may then get sick or die. That is why it is important to drink plenty of water when the weather is hot.

Heat Illnesses

Name	What Is It?	Symptoms
Heatstroke	a life-threatening illness that often occurs when people exercise or are active for a few hours in hot weather; also occurs when people stay for a few days in rooms that are not air-conditioned during hot weather	warm and dry skin, fever that is higher than 104°F (40°C), **nausea**, rapid heartbeat
Heat exhaustion	an illness that can happen before heatstroke	heavy sweating, pale skin, rapid breathing, nausea, headache, fever that is 104°F (40°C) or lower
Heat cramps	an illness that can happen when a person exercises or is physically active in the heat	muscle pains in the hands, calves, feet, thighs, or arms

This chart shows the illnesses people can get when their bodies cannot stay cool. Heat cramps are the least serious illness, and heatstroke is the most serious.

When a person's body is hot, it can sweat out four cups (1 l) of liquid in just an hour.

13

No Escape From the Heat

Sweating keeps people alive in heat waves, but it is often not enough to keep them comfortable. In July 2006, temperatures in Southern California topped 100°F (38°C) for more than a week. It was so hot that Southern California **resident** Terry Payne couldn't sleep. He had no air-conditioning in his bedroom—just a ceiling fan. It wasn't enough to cool the room, so each night he slept in his backyard with his dog.

Pets can get sick from the heat, too. Water and shade can help them beat the heat.

People who did have air-conditioning blasted it night and day. Unfortunately, air conditioners use lots of electricity. Many of California's power systems could not handle the increased demand for electricity. As a result, more than a million people lost power because of **blackouts**.

One Southern California power company reported that nearly one out of every four Southern California customers lost power during the 2006 heat wave.

Refrigerators need electricity to run. When the power went out in California, refrigerators couldn't work, and people's food spoiled.

Operation Cool Down

To help people beat the heat, local California governments launched Operation Cool Down. Some buildings, such as **senior centers**, were turned into cooling centers. People who didn't have air-conditioning at home could relax in the centers' air-conditioned rooms.

People gathering at a cooling center in New York during a heat wave in 2006

Sadly, some people still could not survive the extreme heat. At least 140 Californians died, and many more became ill. Most of the victims were older people. As a person's body ages, it can't cool itself as well as that of a younger person. As a result, older people are especially in danger when it is hot. About 110 of those who died in the California heat wave were over the age of 50.

The cows on this farm were sprayed with water to keep them cool.

Heat waves harm animals as well as humans. The California heat wave killed between 16,000 and 30,000 dairy cows.

When Do Heat Waves Happen?

Heat waves always occur in the summer. During this season, days are longer than at any other time of the year. As a result, the sun has more hours to heat the **atmosphere**. Also, summer nights are shorter than nights in other seasons, so there is less time for air to cool while the sun isn't shining.

Hot days feel even hotter if the **humidity**, or amount of moisture in the air, is high. Why? Sweat cannot easily evaporate when the humidity is high, so it is hard for a person's body to cool off.

If it is sunny a few days in a row, the heat builds up, and each day gets hotter than the one before. When the hot days are 10 degrees Fahrenheit (5 degrees Celsius) hotter than normal, a heat wave occurs. The heat wave will stick around until winds high up in Earth's atmosphere blow the hot air away.

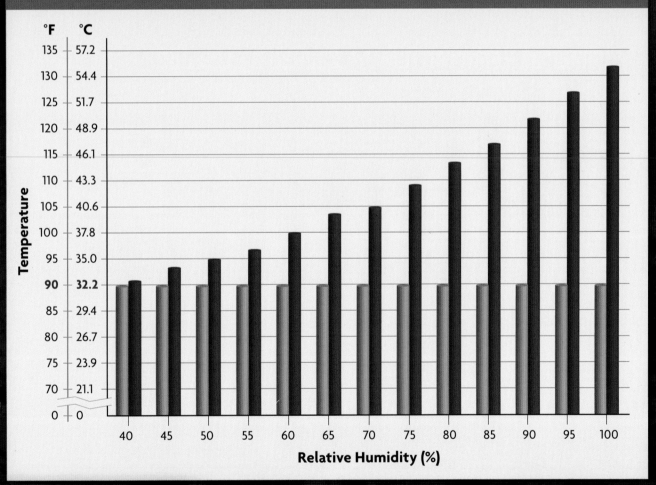

How Hot Does It Feel?

This graph shows how the air temperature on a 90°F (32.2°C) day feels hotter as the humidity increases.

Actual Temperature: 90°F (32.2°C)

How Hot It Feels

The Deadliest Heat Wave

The deadliest heat wave in recent history happened in August 2003 in Europe. August temperatures in European countries such as France usually reach a high of about 70 to 75°F (21 to 24°C). In August 2003, France had nine straight days of temperatures between 95 and 102°F (35 and 39°C).

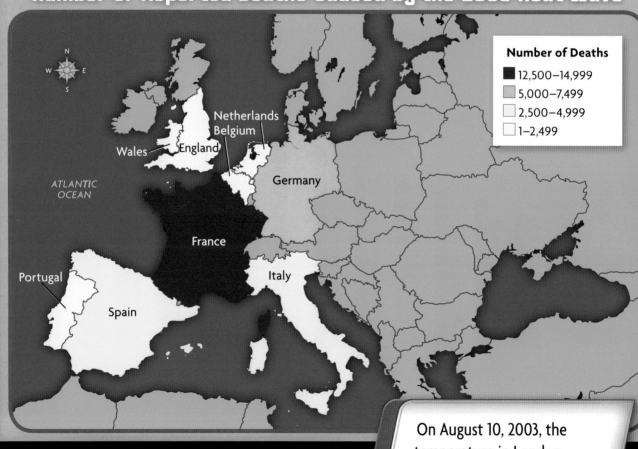

Number of Reported Deaths Caused by the 2003 Heat Wave

Number of Deaths
- 12,500–14,999
- 5,000–7,499
- 2,500–4,999
- 1–2,499

Netherlands
Belgium
Wales England
ATLANTIC OCEAN
Germany
France
Portugal
Italy
Spain

This map shows European countries that reported large numbers of deaths as a result of the 2003 heat wave.

On August 10, 2003, the temperature in London, England, reached 100°F (38°C) for the first time ever.

The intense heat killed about 35,000 people. Paule de Noinville (nwahn-VEE) of France felt lucky to have survived. The 92-year-old woman lived in a **retirement home** that had no air-conditioning. "We in this home are just lucky we had excellent people caring for us," Paule said. Workers gave Paule and others plenty of fluids, wet towels, and ice packs to stay cool. Still, three people in the home died.

During a heat wave in England in 2004, zookeepers at the London Zoo fed penguins fish frozen in ice to keep them cool.

Dangerous Wildfires

The 2003 heat wave in Europe didn't just harm people. It also damaged a lot of land. Very little rain falls during most heat waves. As a result, trees and grass become dry. It then takes very little to start a fire. For example, a spark from the wheel of a train can start a fire in nearby **brush**. In forested areas, **wildfires** can spread and burn thousands of acres.

A wildfire burning in Portugal

During the 2003 heat wave, wildfires across Portugal burned more than 100,000 acres (40,469 hectares) of land in just one week.

More than 500 firefighters battled one wildfire near Silvares, Portugal. Joao Cacoila (zhoh-OW kah-SOY-luh) worried that the blaze would rage into his village. "All we can think about now is protecting our homes," he said. Joao and his home were safe, but others were not so lucky. At least 11 people died in the Portugal blazes.

Firefighters trying to put out wildfires in Portugal

Hotter Than Ever

Scientists expect the number of deadly heat waves to increase in coming years. One reason is that cities continue to grow, and heat waves are hotter and longer in cities. Why? Concrete and dark-colored surfaces **absorb** heat from the sun. Cities have many black streets and lots of buildings with dark rooftops. The buildings are also crowded together, keeping the heat from escaping. Scientists call this the "**urban** heat island effect."

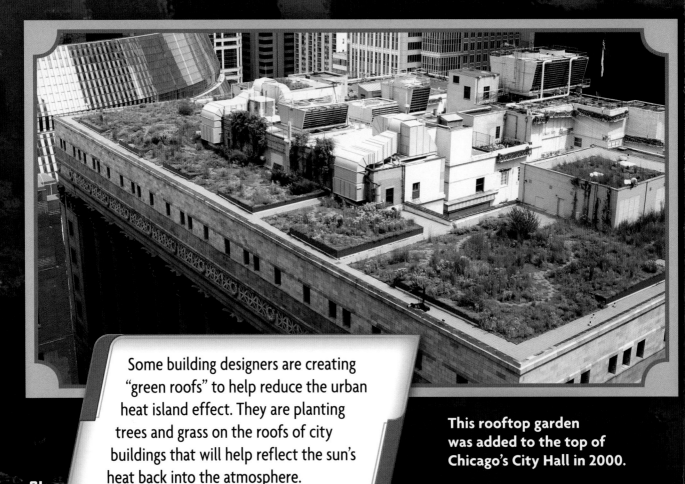

Some building designers are creating "green roofs" to help reduce the urban heat island effect. They are planting trees and grass on the roofs of city buildings that will help reflect the sun's heat back into the atmosphere.

This rooftop garden was added to the top of Chicago's City Hall in 2000.

Some scientists also believe **global climate change** will lead to more heat waves. Some human activities, such as driving cars that burn gasoline, give off **greenhouse gases**. These gases help trap heat in Earth's atmosphere, causing higher temperatures around the world.

Pollution in city air, called smog, can also trap heat.

Preparing For a Warm Future

People around the world are already preparing for future heat waves. In California, power companies are updating their equipment so that they can handle the increased need for electricity during heat waves.

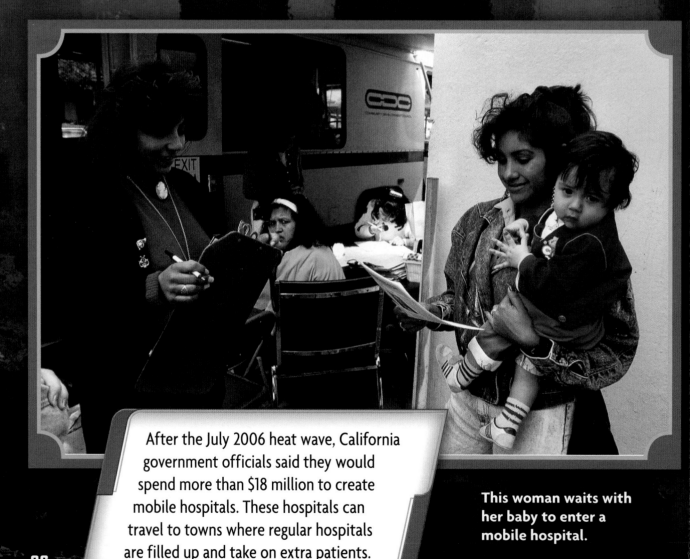

After the July 2006 heat wave, California government officials said they would spend more than $18 million to create mobile hospitals. These hospitals can travel to towns where regular hospitals are filled up and take on extra patients.

This woman waits with her baby to enter a mobile hospital.

Chicago officials have worked hard to avoid another heat disaster. When a heat wave struck in 1999, the city government released strong warnings to city residents about the heat. Police officers checked on older people, and city employees drove people to cooling centers. These efforts kept the number of deaths lower than in 1995. Still, 110 people died. Officials know they can do better. With the right tools to stay cool, even more people will survive the next heat wave.

Chicago officials now post warnings around the city when it is dangerously hot.

Famous Heat Waves

Heat waves have produced deadly results throughout the world. Here are a few of the most famous heat waves in history.

Los Angeles, California, 1955

- One of the deadliest heat waves in the United States took place from August 31 to September 7, 1955, in the Los Angeles area.
- More than 900 people died as a result of the killer temperatures, which topped 100°F (38°C).

India, 2003

- Beginning in May 2003, a month-long heat wave hit India. Temperatures reached as high as 122°F (50°C). The scorching heat and lack of rain led to water shortages.
- The heat killed around 1,500 people.
- The previous year, a heat wave in India had claimed more than 1,000 lives.

Australia, 2009

- In January 2009, extreme heat affected Australia for nearly a week. The temperature reached a blazing 113°F (45°C) in Melbourne.
- The heat caused railroad tracks to bend. More than 50 train rides had to be canceled as a result.

The 2009 heat wave was the worst to hit Australia in a century. Free bottles of water were handed out in some train stations to keep travelers cool.

A dry lake during India's 2003 heat wave

Heat Wave Safety

Here are some heat wave safety tips from the National Weather Service:

- ☑ Protect yourself by staying indoors where there is air-conditioning or some other place that is cool and away from the sun.
- ☑ Do not exercise during the hottest part of the day.
- ☑ Drink plenty of water, even if you are not thirsty.
- ☑ Never leave a pet or child alone in a car or truck. The inside of a vehicle can get very hot and make an animal or person inside ill—and sometimes even cause death.
- ☑ If you go outside, wear loose-fitting clothing, sunscreen, and a hat. White or light-colored clothing is best because it reflects the sun's rays.
- ☑ If you do not have air-conditioning, consider going to a cooling center or the coolest possible place you know, such as a library or movie theater.

Be sure to drink lots of water when it's hot out.

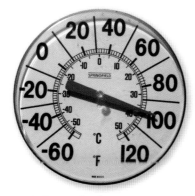

When the heat soars, stay indoors!

Glossary

absorb (ab-ZORB) to soak up something, such as moisture or heat

atmosphere (AT-muhss-*fihr*) the mixture of gases surrounding Earth

blackouts (BLAK-*outs*) periods of time when the electricity in an area fails and the lights go out

brush (BRUSH) an area where small trees and bushes grow

dispatchers (diss-PACH-urhz) operators who send out people, usually in vehicles, to assist others

evaporates (i-VAP-uh-*rayts*) when a liquid such as water changes into a gas

fire hydrants (FIRE HYE-druhnts) outdoor pipes with a spout that water can be taken from

global climate change (GLOH-buhl KLYE-mit CHAYNJ) the warming of Earth's air and oceans due to environmental changes, such as a buildup of greenhouse gases that trap the sun's heat in Earth's atmosphere

greenhouse gases (GREEN-*houss* GAS-iz) carbon dioxide, methane, and other gases that trap warm air in the atmosphere

heat wave (HEET WAYV) very hot weather that lasts for several days

humidity (hyoo-MID-uh-tee) a measure of the water vapor content in the air

meteorologists (*mee*-tee-ur-OL-oh-jists) scientists who study and forecast the weather

nausea (NAW-zhuh) a sick feeling in one's stomach

organs (OR-guhnz) body parts such as the heart or lungs that do a particular job

patients (PAY-shuhnts) people who are being treated by a doctor

resident (REZ-uh-duhnt) a person who lives in a certain place

retirement home (ri-TYE-ur-muhnt HOHM) a place where elderly people who no longer work can live together

senior centers (SEEN-yur SEN-turz) places where elderly people meet to do activities together

shift (SHIFT) a certain period of time when a group of people work

urban (UR-buhn) having to do with a city

wildfires (WILDE-*firez*) fires that spread quickly over a large area, usually in the wilderness

Bibliography

Becerra, Hector. "Southland Heat Wave: It Was a Dark and Sweaty Night." *Los Angeles Times* (July 25, 2006).

Bruni, Frank. "Europe Sizzles and Suffers in a Summer of Merciless Heat." *The New York Times* (August 6, 2003).

Burt, Christopher C. *Extreme Weather: A Guide and Record Book.* New York: W. W. Norton (2007).

Cerveny, Randy. *Freaks of the Storm: From Flying Cows to Stealing Thunder, the World's Strangest True Weather Stories.* New York: Thunder's Mouth Press (2006).

Reiss, Bob. *The Coming Storm: Extreme Weather and Our Terrifying Future.* New York: Hyperion (2001).

Read More

Challen, Paul C. *Drought and Heat Wave Alert!* New York: Crabtree (2005).

Goldstein, Natalie. *Drought and Heat Waves: A Practical Survival Guide.* New York: Rosen (2006).

Learn More Online

To learn more about heat waves, visit
www.bearportpublishing.com/DisasterSurvivors

Index

About the Author

Laura DeLallo has edited dozens of books on history and science over the past 10 years. She now writes children's books and is the editor of an international magazine. She enjoys playing sports and spending time with her cats Quincy and Cesar.